BLESSED PARENTS:
Experiences of
Catholic Parents with
Lesbian and Gay Children

BLESSED PARENTS:
Experiences of Catholic Parents with Lesbian and Gay Children

Edited by
Francis DeBernardo
& Jeannine Gramick, SL

U.S. Publisher: New Ways Ministry
Italian publisher: La Tenda di Gionata

Published in the United States by
New Ways Ministry
4012 29th Street, Mount Rainier, MD 20712
301-277-5674
info@NewWaysMinistry.org
www:NewWaysMinistry.org

Book design by Sister Jeannine Gramick, SL
Cover design by Sister Fran Fasolka, IHM

Library of Congress Control Number: 2021915418

ISBN 978-0-935877-06-9

Keywords: parent, lesbian, gay, queer, religion, Catholic,
sexuality

Acknowledgements

Every publication is the result of contributions of work and advice from many people. Our thanks are extended to all who helped in the Italian edition.

We want to remember:
- the Catholic parents with LGBT children who shared the testimonies of their journey, some of which have been collected in this booklet;
- Gianni Geraci who edited the Italian text and bibliography;
- Giuseppina D'Urso for the revision of the texts;
- Luca Bocchi for graphics and layout;
- don Luca Carrega for the preface;
- don Giovanni Berti for the cartoons that enrich the Italian edition;
-Andrea Diacono, Davide Erbogasto, and Francesco Gagliardi for help in the translation;
-Innocenzo Pontillo for the coordination of the Italian edition.

Dedication

To all the parents in any land over the centuries who struggled to understand their lesbian, gay, bisexual or transgender children and to those who accepted and loved them for the beautiful persons God created them to be.

Table of Contents

Introduction to the English Edition

In October of 1994, New Ways Ministry sponsored the first national Catholic retreat for parents of lesbian and gay people. Sister Jeannine Gramick and Father Robert Nugent, the co-founders of New Ways Ministry, organized the weekend gathering because, by that point in their 23-year ministry to the lesbian/gay community, they saw how isolated and in need of information and spiritual support these parents were. Just like their sons and daughters, the parents were often worried about telling friends, relatives, and parishioners about their family. And sadly, just like their offspring, if they would tell a pastoral minister about their situation, they were often met with a lack of understanding for the challenges and the gifts they experienced. In the worst cases, they were rejected.

So many blessings came from that retreat — and the many more that happened, at least once a year, after that. Instead of feeling like victims, parents became leaders. Simply from the support they gave one another, these mothers and fathers, many of whom had grown up in a church where they were told to "pray, pay, and obey," became the strongest advocates for their children and the LGBTQ community. Blue collar, white collar, and pink collar parents banded together to meet with their pastors, to give talks to their parishes, and to challenge diocesan officials, including bishops. Their advocacy was tireless.

What caused such passion in people who otherwise would have been happy spending their golden years enjoying the simple pleasures of family life? It was a double love: they loved their children and they loved their Church. And they were not willing to give up on either of them. They wanted to bring their children and the Church into a better relationship with each other. So, instead of sitting back on their lawn chairs, they began advocating. They became parents not only to their children, but also to the Church. What is it that a parent does but call the ones they love to be the best that they can be?

The journey of acceptance and love that parents take is the journey that the entire Church must take. Just as parents had to grow to understand sexual orientation and gender identity, and to learn to respect and treasure diversity, so too, does the entire Church. Parents of LGBTQ people are like prophets in the Hebrew Scriptures. Like these ancient advocates, they did not ask for the calling that God gave them, and, at times, that they resisted. But then, just like the Hebrew prophets, they became tireless in calling the religious establishment back to justice and its best ideals.

The stories in this booklet are from Catholic parents not in the U.S., but from Italy. These stories were originally published in Italian by a ministry for Catholic LGBTQ people in Italy called La Tenda di Gionata (Jonathan's Tent). Leaders from this group contacted New Ways Ministry about publishing an English version of their texts. We are proud to do so.

Though half a world away, it is remarkable how these Italian stories reflect the same worries, questions, fears, courage, hope, faith, and love that so many U.S. Catholic parents of LGBTQ people experience on their journeys. From a different culture with different customs, what shines through these stories is the universal love that all parents have for their children.

A famous theological axiom devised by St. Thomas Aquinas says, "Grace builds on nature." I can think of no better example of the truth of this maxim than in reading the stories of Catholic parents of LGBTQ people. The natural love they have for their children has opened them up to an abundance of grace to do remarkable things they would never have dreamed of doing. This grace continues to flower every day as their love, prayers, and efforts are leading the way to renewing the entire Church so that it can become a more equal and just society for all God's children. These are truly "Blessed Parents."

Francis DeBernardo

Preface

There is something prophetic in the pages of this booklet. And we should read prophetic literature by trying to grasp where its signs refer to wider truths. There is no great difference between the prophet Jeremiah who walked around Jerusalem carrying a plow, and a couple of parents dancing at the Pride festival. They are both symbolic acts that call attention to wider issues. They are passionate testimonies of those who do not limit themselves to simply send a message, but also to embody it with their lives. Life flows in the words of these parents who have not given up their roles in complex moments of their family's journey.

These parents of LGBT children call the church and the wider society to be aware of their existence and not treat them and their children as strangers. They do not wish to impose a certain way of thinking, but they do wish to be listened to.

The fact that many have felt so isolated in their time of need is sad and makes us question deeply what it means to be the church. We should be seeking out the lost sheep, those who struggle and feel discriminated against, and yet it seems that not only do we not seek out those in need, but we often push them away from the fold. This kind of pastoral ministry neglects others because seeking out the lost sheep is uncomfortable and frequently provokes resistance from loud and aggressive minorities.

But parents' tenacity is slowly changing things. Many parish priests, catechists, and pastoral workers, who would have difficulty in dealing personally with lesbian and gay people, are starting to explore the issue by meeting with their parents. The perspectives of these church representatives can change significantly, thanks to the patient sharing of these parents. Their support of their children is not just a political act, but an ecclesial act, and the Church should be grateful for it.

The cracks in the wall of marginalization continue to grow, and although our society has a tendency to build barriers to defend itself from everything and everyone, it can't isolate itself from the reality that surrounds it. Even the walls of Jericho fell, and all that was needed was faith *and a trumpet.*

Fr. Gian Luca Carrega

The Stories

A "Blessing" that Changed our Lives

Mara Grassi and Agostino Usai

Now, after ten years, we can say that our son's coming out as gay was a blessing, but at the beginning, and for too long a time, it was difficult and devastating.

We grew up in a country parish where the pastor had spent his life caring for young people and families, cultivating the lofty goals of the Christian life. The particular lofty goals were purity and chastity, nurtured through prayer, confession, spiritual direction, daily communion, and intense and continuous formation. His charisma became concrete as he helped to create communities of couples who helped each other along this path.

Over time, these small communities gave birth to a larger movement of families. We and our friends participated enthusiastically in all the activities in the community. We lived intensely our engagement, marriage, and the birth of our four children.

Almost thirty years after the pastor's death, there is still an educated community to support parents raising their children in the faith. Peer groups, as well as schools, try to help young people accomplish their life projects. With these "holy" families that fostered church vocations, we considered ourselves very fortunate and thought there was no better environment for ourselves and our children than this one.

So, in such an environment, discovering that we had a homosexual son was more explosive than a bomb.

We found that there was no place for those who, for whatever reason, were different.

Homosexuality was not even thought of. It was a problem that didn't concern us and it had never been a topic of reflection. Because our community thought that there were no homosexuals among us, it was acceptable to think their behavior was depraved and unnatural.

But we began to ask ourselves, "Is this right? Is it right that parish communities and other church movements that seek to follow Christ in a 'way of perfection' exclude those who do not fall within the social standards of what is considered 'normal'? Didn't Christ die for everyone?"

When our son turned to some of the priests in our lay movement for help about a part of himself that he could no longer deny, he felt judged, interrogated and, in a word, "wrong." These negative reactions caused him to distance himself from our family movement, from the Church, and finally, unfortunately, from the faith.

We parents went to the same priests and, of course, were told that we should continue to love him. But we would always leave those talks with the feeling that what had happened to us was the greatest suffering and misfortune that God could have sent us.

We could have accepted so much, but not that our son was gay! But one set of friends, a deacon and his wife, made us reflect on the absurdity of such ideas. They helped us understand what, after all, we always felt in our hearts: that we had to put the love that we owed to our son before everything else.

As time went by, our hearts lightened, even
though we had to accept his move to the city. The country
situation was suffocating him. He could no longer bear the
pain he read on his mother's face, even though she tried to
hide it. In the meantime, he began therapy, which helped
him not to 'heal' or change his orientation (as, at first,
mother had hoped), but to accept his homosexuality.

We lived this way for ten years. Relationships in
the family had become more serene. As husband and wife,
we grew closer. But in the parish and with the families of
our lay movement, a "curtain of silence" had fallen. Everyone knew our son was gay, but nobody, not even the
priests, would talk or ask about it. So a distance developed
between us and those in the parish and lay movements.

Instinctively we rebelled against the idea of a God
who is not the father of all His children. We rejected the
notion of a Church that denies salvation to those who
simply want to be themselves, and denies them the chance
to concretely love another person. We tried tenaciously to
continue our life of faith even if this new way of being
Christian slowly distanced us from the families of which
we were a part.

We still now feel united with the friends with
whom we shared forty years of life. We do not allow ourselves to judge their silence because we realize that we
ourselves had never talked about our son. If we hadn't
needed to come to terms with his homosexual orientation,
we would still be the most reactionary of Christians.

Our life started to change dramatically in May
2017 when we participated in the prayer vigil against
homophobia that was organized in Regina Pacis Parish, in
Reggio Emilia. We discovered that the parish hosted a
group of LGBT Catholics that also included parents. By

chance (we are convinced that Providence makes use of chance), we discovered the Gruppo Davide (David Group) in Parma, which supports Catholic parents with lesbian and gay children.

Through learning and sharing with other parents and with members of LGBT Christian groups, we started to understand that our son's homosexuality was not a misfortune that happened to us, but rather it was a gift. We discovered that parents are also the victims of homophobia when they fail to love and accept their children in their diversity. All children are different. All are unique and must be respected in the fullness of their truth. Parents are victims of homophobia when they feel judged or pitied by those around them, or when they feel guilty or ashamed of their child because of a different sexual orientation.

We now know that we have been blessed to have a gay child because this forced us to change our mentality and our way of living the faith. Our Catholic life was seemingly perfect. We had respected all the rules. We thought we had all the answers until life changed the questions. Life is never a straight road; it is full of surprises that suddenly intrude and require us to be open to whatever is coming. The only answer was and remains love. Love is greater than our miseries, our past, our mistakes, our judgments, our fears, and the certainty of having failed.

"God is greater than our heart" (1 John 3:20). Instead of trying to find someone to blame, or to nurture feelings of guilt, our heart simply had to be open to a grateful discovery, not allowing doubt or fear to substitute for the face of God. "Whoever loves is begotten of God and knows God" (1 John 4: 7). If you know all the rules, all the precepts, but do not love, you do not know God.

We work now with other parents who share and understand what we went through. We work so that no one will be excluded from society and from the Church because of sexual orientation. We feel one with Jesus in whom "there is no longer Jew nor Greek, neither slave nor free, neither male nor female, neither pure nor impure" (Gal 3:28). It is a new path in which we do not have the certainties that we had before, but we think that the joy we are living shows that the path is right and that we are walking well. If you love, you will bear fruit, perhaps not immediately, but the fruit, even if it is late, will come.

Remembering that no one can be excluded from the Kingdom of God by living the truth, we close with an excerpt from a hymn from the Monastery of Bose, an ecumenical community:

> *O Lord, who traces the path*
> *and opens the doors of the Kingdom,*
> *renew our hope*
> *so that every life may make sense. Amen.*

Postscript:

On September 16, 2020, Pope Francis received a group of forty representatives from La Tenda di Gionata (Jonathan's Tent) at the Vatican. After the audience, the vice president of the association, Mara Grassi, and her husband, Agostino Usai, presented Pope Francis with a copy of GENITORI FORTUNATI, the Italian book of this English translation.

They also gave the Pontiff letters with requests and stories about how the LGBT community has been treated by the Church. Pope Francis graciously received them and said, "The Church does not exclude them. It loves your children as they are because they are children of God."

Pope Francis smiled as he received a rainbow t-shirt with the words, "In love there is no fear" (1 John 4:18). Mara Grassi said this was a moment of "deep harmony that we will not forget."

The group also released a video of parents' testimonies, with English subtitles, listed in the resource section of this book.

The Time My Son Told Me
"I'm in Love with a Guy"

Dea Santonico

It was Saturday, May 7th, 2016. A special evening awaited us. Our son, Marco, and his girlfriend, Laura, invited us to dinner at a restaurant. It was not just any place. It was the restaurant where they would have their wedding reception. Their wedding was just two months away and they wanted to share an evening with us beside Lake Martignano.

We arrived at sunset. First, a stroll in the nearby meadow and later dinner at a table for five for the whole family: Marco and Laura, us parents, and our other son, Emanuele. It was a special dinner and a charming place, too. We headed back to the car, thinking that this lovely evening was ending there.

The five of us got into the car, with the younger adults sitting in the back. Before we left, my son, Emanuele, who was seated behind me, said, "I have some good news – at least for me it's good. I've been seeing a guy for two months, his name is G. I knew for some time…"

He knew, but we didn't. None of us even suspected as much. That was his good news, uttered with fear in his heart that it would not have been as good for us. Silence descended on us for a long time, but then I broke the silence.

"Emanuele, I have to give you a hug." When I got out of the car and opened the back door, he was in tears,

and that scene left me speechless. His sob had let out all
the pain that was hidden for years. It was also a sob of an
ever-growing sense of freedom. He succeeded in sharing
with us a weight that he had carried alone for a long time.
We embraced each other. I could feel the pain and everything else running through my body. Then his dad embraced him and so did Marco and Laura. No words can
describe our feelings in that moment.

"Now I need ten minutes alone. I'll be back,"
Emanuele said, and he walked away in the dark. After a
moment's hesitation, my other son, Marco, joined him. I
have always been moved by their relationship with each
other ever since Emanuele was five years old and waited
eagerly for his little brother to come out of my tummy.

The rest of us stayed in the car. Without even no-
ticing it, we held each other's hands. I looked at my husband and caressed him. I knew it would not be easy for
him.

As soon as Marco and Emanuele returned, we left.
"Now focus on your thesis and graduation. We have to
grow on this together," his father told Emanuele. I thought
it was the most beautiful thing his father could have told
him. It was very simple and very true.

That evening I gave birth to Emanuele for a second time. I could feel the power of life emerging from the
pain that was flowing and rushing through my entire
body. This is my recollection of that evening several years
ago.

Other memories inhabit the hearts of the others
who lived through that experience. Those seated in the
back of the car recalled the emotional expression on
Emanuele's face while he spoke. Others remembered the
warm hugs that followed. The silence seemed to me very

long but others did not notice the silence. Emanuele still calls to mind the words uttered by his father, "Even I want to hug my son." Others remember the moment the two brothers spent together when they walked away from the car.

We returned to Lake Martignano two months later, on July 9th for a Eucharistic celebration on the shores of the lake. Marco and Laura pledged their love for each other as we witnessed the exchange of their wedding vows. To put yourself out there and disclose your feelings is hard. It requires courage and has an infectious effect. On the shore of the lake that day, we all put ourselves out there, looked inwards, and overcame the fear of disclosing our feelings. Even Emanuele had the courage to speak these beautiful words:

"Love is beautiful. It seems like a truism but I think we often forget it, or want to forget it, or we want to push it aside so as not to see it. I would like to thank Marco and Laura because today they are expressing their love, sharing it with us and putting it out there for all to see. And in the event that there exists a creator, I think he threw a glance at the shores of this lake and smiled, pleased with his creation."

Yes, God was there that day on Lake Martignano. And He was there too, that evening two months before, beside Emanuele. It was the same God who had heard the anguished cry of an enslaved people and stood at their side to set them free from their slavery on a risky journey toward freedom. Even Emanuele had an anguished cry to let out and chains to break that hindered him from living his truth. Emanuele was beginning to be open about his feelings and disclosing that part of himself that hypocritical and self-righteous people would prefer that he keep hidden.

Later in the same month as the wedding, Emanuele graduated and received his degree in Engineering. In the acknowledgments of his degree thesis, he wrote:

The university studies and the journey of life are bound to intertwine. This is true for us all. In my case, they often strangled each other; but at the end many knots are finally being untangled. For this, I would like to thank my family for their constant love, for their support, and for all that they would have given me had I been able to ask for it.

A word of thanks to all those who stood by me and guided me when I was most in need. You are my strength. Thank you to all those who believed in me and knew how to love me, even when I was unable to love myself. You are my pride and joy. Thanks to those who, despite everything, were able to show me beauty in those places where I was unable to find it.

Last but not least, I am grateful to all those who see me as I really am and still continue to see me with the same eyes. You have taught me the true meaning of the word "grace." For without some grace, there's nowhere to go.

Thank you, Emanuele, for gifting us that moment. Let that beauty which you were able to find inside you shine in its entirety and in such a way as to enlighten your life and that of others. That way God the Creator, the same God you had a glimpse of on the shores of Lake Martignano, may gaze at your life and smile, pleased with His creation.

A Network of Love and Care

Marisa Delmonte, Angelo Donati, and Silvia Donati

We, Marisa and Angelo, are the happy grandparents of five grandchildren, including Nicola, a 20-year-old young man who is gay. Nicola's life made us feel dubious and anxious, but we wanted to let our emotions evolve and develop so we could gain a better understanding of all we were experiencing.

Our daughter, Silvia, noticed our trepidation. With humility, simplicity, and considerable love, she guided us to understand better and to embrace our grandson, and for this we are grateful. We shared in Nicola's fears, his loneliness, and the painful rejection by his classmates that compelled him to change school twice. Nicola was obviously not accepted by his peers. He was marginalized and made an object of ridicule.

But our family formed a network of love, warmth, and care for him. Our complete acceptance was a great support for Nicola. We strengthened him to overcome considerable difficulties. Even his cousins accepted him with maturity and spontaneity that astounded us adults.

We usually spend our summer in the mountains, and our children and grandchildren often come to visit us. Even Nicola used to come to the mountains.

During one summer at the mountains, Nicola met another gay student of his age with whom he established an intimate and positive friendship. Their bonding with each other helped them to reconcile themselves with the world that had made them feel excluded. This relationship became love, a reciprocal gift for each other, and their happiness was passed on to us. This made us feel very content.

We have always prayed for Nicola, placing him at the foot of the cross, entrusting him to the Lord, and invoking God's blessing. Nicola is the "Church." He is loved and cherished by God just the way he is, just like the rest of us. We are confident that God will protect, console, and guide him in life.

Pope Francis' reflections on homosexuality fill us with hope because they break the shame and taboo surrounding this topic. Pope Francis shows us how to love our neighbor according to the Gospel.

Nonetheless, it pains us to see how a certain worldview and entrenched traditions generate exclusive attitudes that continue to persist in the Church, an institution that should be a mother to all. However, we believe that Jesus is with us along the way of life, no matter the length of our journey. And Jesus is with Nicola and our family.

A Benevolent Gaze

Corrado Contini and Michela Munari

As we read and reflected on Fr. James Martin's book, *Building a Bridge*, the image that came to mind was that of the old bridge in Merano that spans the Passirio River in northernmost Italy. The bridge reminded us of the new relationship between the Church and LGBT persons. We would like to share our belief, particularly with the parents of LGBT children, that "We parents can be and are, in fact, an important arch of that bridge."

But how? How can we help priests and our children come together and walk that two-lane bridge that requires both groups to undertake the journey? We came out of our closet and acknowledged the fact that we parents are blessed with "different" children. This realization opened up new horizons for us. We parents now have the possibility of helping our children heal from their psychological, spiritual, and physical wounds. At the same time, we can help our priests see our children with new eyes.

A benevolent gaze is indeed essential. This benevolent gaze is an outlook that is able to catch sight of the good that is present in life. A benevolent gaze is a fresh perspective that can notice the hidden goodness one cannot see and to which one may be oblivious. A benevolent gaze is a frame of mind that can help us express and accomplish the best of our potential, to feel good, and feel at home. It makes us feel whole, authentic, and precious.

An attitude of benevolence does not infantilize persons but gives them wings to fly. It helps and supports

a person's responsible choices of all that is good, true, and
beautiful in life. This way of thinking is the same benevolent gaze of our Heavenly Father who looks at us with
eyes of goodness. It is a gaze of love that called us into being from eternity.

> *You formed my inmost being;*
> *You knit me in my mother's womb.*
> *I praise you, because I am wonderfully made;*
> *Wonderful are your works!*
> *My very self you know.*
> -Psalm 139, 13-14

By adopting this new way of seeing, our priests
can undertake the journey of reconciliation. It is only
through new eyes that they can help our LGBT children
step out of the shadow while also recognizing the gifts
they are able to bring to the Church. Only with this approach are priests able to see our children as beloved children of God while also perceiving the unfair discrimination to which they are subject. Only with this attitude are
priests able to listen to them, to draw closer to them, and
even to suffer with them. Only with the eyes of the heart
can they become aware of the other's spirit and state of
mind. It is through this benevolent gaze that our bishops
and priests can practice respect, compassion, and sensitivity required of them in their ministry.

We also urge our children to adopt this approach.
They have to overcome their resentment and eradicate the
mentality of 'us' vs. 'them.' Within the Church, there
should not exist 'us' and 'them' because Jesus taught us
that we are all children of God, forgiven and welcomed as
we are. With the eyes of the heart, we hope that our children are able to treat those who have different views with
respect, while also upholding their own positions in a serene and prudent manner. This approach will help them

have compassion for the Church and its teaching, to be mindful of the weight of the bishops' duties and responsibilities, to take into consideration the humanity of the bishops, and to give our Church leaders time to learn and understand their reality.

We want to accompany each other in this quest and adventure and, in doing so, affirm that every life is worthy and deserves to be lived fully. Pope Francis' words in *Evangelii Gaudium* ring out loud:

"Those wounded by historical divisions find it difficult to accept our invitation to forgiveness and reconciliation, since they think that we are ignoring their pain or are asking them to give up their memory and ideals (par. 100). ... Let us ask the Lord to help us understand the law of love. How good it is to have this law! How much good it does us to love one another, in spite of everything. Yes, in spite of everything! (par. 101)"

It is through the law of mutual love, which is benevolent gazing, and the openness of heart, with the building blocks of respect, compassion, and sensitivity that the two-lane bridge can be built. This is a bridge to which we parents are called to be an important arch. This is a bridge that will emerge as beautiful and wonderful as the Medieval Romanesque bridge of Merano in northern Italy.

A Day of a Thousand Colors

Serenella Longarini and Salvatore Olmetto

On July 7, 2018, we took part in our first-ever Pride March in Bologna with a group of LGBT Catholics. We had many misconceptions about the parade because we assumed it would be quite excessive and, at times, obscene. However, we learned along the way that we need to give up our prejudices and allow ourselves to be amazed by the world around us.

At the Pride parade, we initially felt like fish out of water. The hubbub, the colors, the enthusiasm of the crowds in the celebration—all of this seemed to drag us in like a wave in the sea. We were moved especially by many young people who, in our estimation, had a tremendous desire to cry out to the world and say,"I am here! I exist! I need to love and, above all, be loved!"

As parents, we yearned to embrace them all, to hold them in our arms, and to cuddle them in an attempt to heal the wounds in their hearts. Sadly, we know there are many, many gashes they have received--too many.

This festival experience made us understand that a Pride event is not excessive. On the contrary, it is our own judgments, our respectability, and our moral legalism that are excessive. They serve as masks by which we hide our inability to welcome and accept others unconditionally.

We were struck by the fact that the banner carried by LGBT Christians attracted so much attention. We, who have been catechists for a long time, felt the joy and enthusiasm of being able to evangelize and share God's love in this way. We would like to have shouted loudly to all the young people present, "God, our Creator, is here and God loves you just as you are!"

Yet, we did shout from our hearts in the midst of so much noise. Through our presence at the parade, we wanted to convey exactly this message, not only to LGBT persons but also, above all, to the many parents who still struggle to accept their children just the way they are-- their wonderful sons and daughters.

Together with other parents, we thought that it would be a beautiful idea to attend Pride parades in the following years to show our pride and the honor we feel in being Catholic parents of LGBT children. We want to show the world our gratitude to God for blessing us with such wonderful sons and daughters. Perhaps we shall dance a little less, but only because we are no longer young enough to do certain things!

The Gift of Coming Out

Andrea Baghi and Silvia Donati

On July 19, 2013, our second-born son, Nicola, gifted us with his coming out. He was almost 15 years old. We remember that day very well. It was the anniversary of the Via d'Amelio bombing, when Paolo Borsellino, a brave Sicilian magistrate, was killed in a terrorist attack organized by the Mafia. It may seem a daring comparison, but I like to compare Nicola's courage to this modern hero, Borsellino.

Nicola was young, but he challenged everything and everyone. He was tired of being mocked and excluded, of pretending and hiding, and he decided to throw away the mask to reveal his true face, getting rid of a burden he could not bear anymore. "Yes, I am gay. I can finally tell you, because I don't want to hide any more."

For Nicola, that was an important gesture, as well as being deeply painful and troubling. In fact, Nicola was very concerned about disappointing or hurting us, but he did not catch us unprepared. We, his parents, saw it coming for a long time. We expected it, and eventually we encouraged and accompanied him in taking this step.

Ever since he was a child, we could see that he was different. We could see it when he played, in the way he reacted to his friends, and in all the ways he expressed his personality. So very gradually, we became ready to accept his homosexuality, as much as possible, with love, openness, and availability.

For many years, with some difficulty and fear in the secrecy of our hearts, we treasured who he was. We learned to love Nicola's true self and let it emerge. His most authentic and deepest identity was like a fragile plant that tries to grow in a dry, hostile, and dangerous environment. We made sure to cultivate in ourselves and in our family, a beautiful, positive, and normal image of being gay so that our son could see himself in that image, and experience around him an atmosphere of trust, support, and affection.

The day of coming out, which many young people fear, was beautiful, serene, and spontaneous for Nicola. He announced his truth with the courage and determination of his young age. And we, his parents, were excited and accepted his gift for we had not taken it for granted. We were happy to be able to be part of his new life, ready to accompany him and support him in the long and difficult journey of growing and maturing.

Since then, our lives have changed a lot. The world of the LGBT Catholic community opened up to us. This is a world we didn't know existed, and it has become our world too. It is a difficult and bumpy journey, but so rich in humanity.

After Nicola's coming out, we came out as well, as parents of an LGBT child. We came out to our families, friends, and to the church community we have belonged to for a long time. We wanted to share our experience as parents who regard their child's homosexuality not as a disgrace, with guilt or shame, but rather as a normal and different strand of human sexuality. His coming out was not a tragedy but a chance to experience a richer life and to grow personally and as a family.

An important consequence of our coming out was meeting other parents of LGBT children. We built a community with them, that includes other LGBT Catholics. For the past few years, this group has become a valuable opportunity for us to share, grow, and support each other. In our society and in the Catholic community, we parents often experience misunderstanding and indifference, sometimes refusal and even hostility. We often feel frustrated that we cannot realize the dream of a world where discrimination based on sexual orientation is a thing of the past.

We wish our children and their partners could live their lives in freedom and truth. But we do not give up. We keep faith with the promise to stand by our child's side, to stand with all LBGT people, to share their journey, to develop a society more welcoming towards different people and, most of all, to remind our children they are wonderful just as they are.

My Child Is Gay?
Let's Talk about It

Gianni Geraci

In October 1997, the *Committee for Marriage and Family of the United States Conference of Catholic Bishops* published the letter *Always Our Children,* a pastoral message to parents with lesbian or gay children. The letter also included suggestions for pastoral workers. It is an important document and starts from the observation that many lesbian and gay people come from average Catholic families. It recognizes how the pain suffered by parents and the spiritual growth that can arise from a child's coming out can represent an important challenge in the life of these families.

One of the sections of the document summarizes the emotions that parents experience when they discover that their children are lesbian or gay. The letter acknowledges the fact that Catholic teaching on homosexuality can be a source of conflict for them. It is a summary that is certainly the fruit of careful listening to the concrete experience of many Catholic parents who had to come to terms with the homosexuality of their children.

For this reason, it is appropriate to report this passage from the letter in full at the beginning of this brief essay.

Because some of you might be swept up in a tide of emotions, we focus first on feelings. Although the gift of human sexuality can be a great mystery at times, the Church's teaching on homosexuality is clear. However, because the terms of that teaching have now become very personal in regard to your son or daughter, you may feel confused and conflicted. You could be experiencing many different emotions, all in varying degrees, such as the following:

Relief. Perhaps you had sensed for some time that your son or daughter was different in some way. Now he or she has come to you and entrusted something very significant. It may be that other siblings learned of this before you and were reluctant to tell you. Regardless, though, a burden has been lifted. Acknowledge the possibility that your child has told you this not to hurt you or create distance, but out of love and trust and with a desire for honesty, intimacy, and closer communication.

Anger. You may be feeling deceived or manipulated by your son or daughter. You could be angry with your spouse, blaming him or her for "making the child this way" — especially if there has been a difficult parent-child relationship. You might be angry with yourself for not recognizing indications of homosexuality. You could be feeling disappointment, along with anger, if family members, and sometimes even siblings, are rejecting their homosexual brother or sister. It is just as possible to feel anger if family members or friends seem overly accepting and encouraging of homosexuality. Also — and not to be discounted — is a possible anger with God that all this is happening.

Mourning. You may now feel that your child is not exactly the same individual you once thought you knew. You envision that your son or daughter may never give you grandchildren. These lost expectations as well as the fact that homosexual persons often encounter discrimination and open hostility can cause you great sadness.

Fear. You may fear for your child's physical safety and general welfare in the face of prejudice against homosexual people. In particular, you may be afraid that others in your community might exclude or treat your child or your family with contempt. The fear of your child contracting HIV/AIDS or another sexually transmitted disease is serious and ever-present. If your child is distraught, you may be concerned about attempted suicide.

Guilt, Shame, and Loneliness. "If only we had...or had not..." are words with which parents can torture themselves at this stage. Regrets and disappointments rise up like ghosts from the past. A sense of failure can lead you into a valley of shame which, in turn, can isolate you from your children, your family, and other communities of support.

Parental Protectiveness and Pride. Homosexual persons often experience discrimination and acts of violence in our society. As a parent, you naturally want to shield your children from harm, regardless of their age. You may still insist: "You are always my child; nothing can ever change that. You are also a child of God, gifted and called for a purpose in God's design."

There are two important things to keep in mind as you try to sort out your feelings. First, listen to them. They can contain clues that lead to a fuller discovery of God's will for you. Second, because some feelings can be confusing or conflicting, it is not necessary to act upon all of them. Acknowledging them may be sufficient, but it may also be necessary to talk about your feelings. Do not expect that all tensions can or will be resolved. The Christian life is a journey marked by perseverance and prayer. It is a path leading from where we are to where we know God is calling us.

If the news of a child's homosexuality catches a parent unexpectedly, a normal reaction is to experience something similar to a period of mourning. We may think that the person who was there before is not there anymore, and in his or her place there is a stranger. So it is normal for a parent to go through negative and painful moods. The important thing, however, is to make the right choices even when emotions and feelings may be pessimistic and negative.

The homosexuality of children is not primarily about parents. It is not something they "did to you." They did not "choose" to have a "homosexual lifestyle" to rebel against you or to make you unhappy. Try to see it from their eyes to truly understand it.

When they decide to tell you about their sexual orientation, they are already quite sure of it. They almost certainly lived alone with this awareness for a long time. They observed their peers and they realized they were not developing the same feelings as others. Maybe they even tried to have relationships with people of the opposite sex to see if something could begin, but they had to take note of the fact that nothing did. So when they come out to you, they have likely already trodden a long path. Avoid asking them if they are sure, if maybe they want to take some time, or if they want to see what happens. Instead, take into account the journey they have made, and tell them how grateful you are for the courage they have had to finally talk to you about such a delicate topic.

In coming out, your children have overcome their fear because they know that the discovery of homosexuality often brings coldness, threats, and exclusion. Be proud of them. You have strong children who, trusting you, have given you the opportunity to re-create a confidence that was in danger of being lost.

You did not cause the homosexuality of your children. Do not listen to those who claim that homosexuality in men is caused by an absent father or an excessively present mother. If this were true, more men would be gay because many remember this kind of parental dynamics.

Susan Cottrell wrote on her blog, "When I was young, I thought that the cause of homosexuality was a trauma suffered during childhood. To my surprise, God radically changed my idea and introduced me to many people who had wonderful childhoods and who, despite this, have a homosexual orientation. He also introduced me to many others who had a traumatic childhood and, despite this, remained heterosexual."[1]

A mistake many parents often make is attributing the origin of their child's homosexuality to "bad company." Your child is not homosexual because of hanging out with certain gay or lesbian friends. If anything, the reason he or she is with such friends is precisely because of their shared sexual orientation. If there is a romantic relationship, parents often blame the other person for manipulating their child and for pushing him or her towards homosexuality. Parents try to prevent their children from spending time with these acquaintances. Yet, the only result is making them suffer unnecessarily and creating an atmosphere of tension and conflict that block any form of trust and confidence.

The Catechism of the Catholic Church says that a person's homosexuality is "deeply rooted" (n. 2358). Try to travel down memory lane to revisit your own youth. Many of the things you were convinced of back then no longer form part of your beliefs, but among the things that have not changed over time, almost certainly, is your sexual orientation. So do not expect that you can impose a specific life path on your children.

---

[1] Susan Cottrell, the author of the book, *Mom, I'm Gay: Loving Your LGBTQ Child Without Sacrificing Your Faith*, (Austin, Freedhearts Publishing, 2013) lives in Texas and has five children, two of whom are lesbian. See *To Christian Parents of Gay Children*, 2013, freedhearts.wordpress.com/2013/06/10/to-the-parents-of-gay-children.

Do not deceive them by telling them that the attraction they feel for people of the same sex is associated with a particular phase of life that will surely pass. Instead, try to recognize their path. Now that they have confided their sexual orientation with you, you can finally accompany them along the journey that lies ahead of them. If, at some point, they realize that they have a different orientation than the one they shared with you, they will notice it themselves. Remember that telling them that you are praying for them to change or to 'fall in line' when they grow up risks alienating your children further from you.

Do not push them to attend one of those groups that claim they can change a person's sexual orientation. Experience shows us that the paths proposed by these groups only traumatize people and reinforce a deep sense of shame and self-loathing that constitute one of the biggest risks faced by lesbian and gay persons.

Paolo Rigliano, a psychotherapist, has observed, "It is necessary to recognize that with homosexuality, even today, processes converge and unfold in a unique way... Homosexual persons find that no one wants them to be that way. In the vast majority of cases, they feel they are 'something they should not have been,' something they feel guilty about, like a physical impairment. They too see themselves as unexpected. A vast amount of research shows they did not envision or desire their sexuality, even those who discover themselves as gay at a later stage of-life.[2]

---

[2] Rigliano P., Ciliberto J., Ferrari F., Curare i gay? Oltre l'ideologia riparativa dell'omosessualità, Raffaello Cortina, Milano, 2011, pp. 17-20. I am unable to quote this text in full but I recommend this publication to the reader.

Remember that Jesus does not ask you to change your children but to love them and to help them. Through your love for them, discover the greatness of God's love. During the general audience of September 13, 1978, Pope John Paul I invited those present to recite a prayer that was particularly meaningful to him. It is a prayer that can help you deal with the negative effects of fearing a change in your life. "Lord, take me as I am, with all my faults and shortcomings, but help me become as you desire me to be!" His words remind us that the path of conversion we are called to pursue entails the full acceptance of our own humanity, including those aspects of our humanity we dislike.

If you think the life your child will live after coming out is not what you dreamed of, remember that God is perhaps asking you to accept this way of life to make manifest His love in the midst of so much anger and hatred. Perhaps God intends to use your witness to restore His name in those places where contempt and fear have smeared the divine face. Spiritual literature is full of examples whereby God confronts us with unexpected situations to move us out of our narrow worldview. God shakes everything that can be shaken and, in this way, helps us to discover what really matters and is essential. Cling to God in this life, and God will lead you towards something wonderful for yourself, for your children, and for your family.

Embrace your children when they confide their homosexuality to you. Just imagine the courage they had to muster to tell you about it, maybe aware that they were telling you something that is not suited to the family's value system. At the moment of their coming out, your children need to know they did the right thing. You may be overwhelmed with fear, doubt, anger, pain, disappointment, shame, anguish, or guilt, but do not let these emotions prevent you from expressing your unconditional love for them. They already have to face their own emotions.

Don't burden them with your emotions, too. Give yourself time to understand and process the moods and emotions triggered by the discovery of your child's homosexuality. However, while working on emotional changes, make your love known to your children in the simplest and most emphatic way by embracing them for a long time and letting them know that your love as parents is even greater than before.

Afterword to the English Edition

When Father Robert Nugent and I first met Catholic lesbian and gay people in Philadelphia in 1971, we heard horrific stories of parents rejecting many of them. More to be pitied than condemned, these parents were following the social conventions and distorted thinking of the time and the religious judgmentalism of their Church. But over the years, we met scores and scores of parents who rejected the harsh customs and rules they had been taught. They loved their children while also loving the Church that had formed their families.

Fr. Nugent and I knew that we needed to reach out to these parents who suffered because of their two loves. We had to let them know that they could hold both loves close to their hearts. New Ways Ministry, the organization we co-founded, began holding retreats for parents. One early and very memorable retreat was facilitated by Bishop Thomas Gumbleton, an auxiliary bishop of Detroit, who shared his story about the letter that his brother, Dan, sent to the whole family, letting them know about his gay identity.

The parents at the retreat resonated with the bishop's numbness and inability to talk to his brother or family when he first received Dan's letter. He couldn't share his feelings because there was often a deadness inside. Then there were nagging questions. At the retreat he confessed his own homophobia to the parents. What would the other bishops say when they found out his brother was gay? Would they think he himself was gay too? For a whole year he thought and prayed, struggled and searched the Scriptures. Very gradually, he realized that Dan was the same person he had grown up with and loved, except now he knew that Dan was gay and he realized that God had created him that way.

On one of his visits to his mother, as Bishop Gumbleton was saying good-bye at the door of her home, she turned to him and asked, "Tom, is Dan going to hell?" Without hesitation, the bishop replied, "No, mother, of course not... God made Dan that way and God doesn't send us to hell because of who we are." Through his months of prayer, Bishop Gumbleton had had a conversion. He believed that God wanted Dan and his partner to be happy the way they were and to share love profoundly and intimately with each other.

Many parents nodded their heads because they had experienced similar epiphanies with their own children. Most of them had come to the same conclusion: God loved their gay or lesbian children just as they were, and these children were not going to hell because they had a partner. But hearing these words from a bishop helped them to reconcile their two loves: their children and their Church.

Over the years Father Nugent and I met so many caring and faith-filled parents like those at the retreats. We encouraged them to reach out to other parents and to form mutual support groups. One set of parents, Casey and Mary Ellen Lopata, stand out because they devoted decades of their lives to ministry on behalf of other struggling parents. After meeting with their bishop, they worked in conjunction with the Family Life Office in their home diocese of Rochester, New York. Their tireless work gradually evolved into Fortunate Families, a national network for parents seeking justice and equality for LGBT persons and their families.

In addition to encouraging Catholic parents to tell their stories to Church leaders, Casey and Mary Ellen promoted a "Listening Parents Network" of more than 100 parents. Besides fielding phone calls and email messages from Catholic parents who needed safe and confidential conversations, some of the listening parents joined in public advocacy for marriage equality before the U.S. Supreme Court decision legalized same-sex marriage. From 1992 until their retirement in 2014, Casey and Mary Ellen provided compassionate ministry, personal witness, and national leadership in serving the needs of parents and families with LGBT children. Fortunate Families continues today to support Catholic LGBTQ+ sisters and brothers, their families, friends, and allies.

I feel a deep affection for Casey and Mary Ellen and for all the devoted parents I have met. Their questions are similar to those of the Italian parents in this book. Did we do something wrong? Why didn't my son or daughter tell me sooner? How can we come out in our parish? Why doesn't the Church fully welcome my child?

Several of the Italian parents are also interviewed in a short video regarding their feelings and experiences when they learned about their children's sexual orientation. After sharing how their families dealt with this knowledge, they give some advice to parents who have just found out their child is gay or lesbian. I highly recommend watching this ten-minute YouTube video. Not to worry: it has English subtitles!

I urge you to plunge into the books, videos, and U.S. organizations listed as resources in the following pages. But please remember that the greatest resource available to you to understand sexual orientation and sexual diversity is the love you have for your own child. Love shows us the way!

Jeannine Gramick, SL

Resources

Catholic Bibliography

Books

Alison, James. *Faith Beyond Resentment: Fragments Catholic and Gay.* New York: Crossroad, 2001. An examination of the Scriptures to help the reader move beyond resentment against oppressors, including oppressors of LGBTQ people.

Boswell, John. *Christianity, Social Tolerance and Homosexuality.* Chicago: University of Chicago Press, 1980. A ground-breaking historical account of gay history that shows how and why periods of tolerance and oppression occurred.

Boswell, John. *Same Sex Unions in Pre-Modern Europe.* New York: Villard, 1994. A history of ancient and medieval commitment ceremonies between people of the same gender, with some sources from the Vatican archives.

DeBernardo, Francis. *Mychal Judge: 'Take Me Where You Want Me to Go.'* Collegeville, Minnesota: Liturgical Press, 2022. A spiritual biography of the gay Franciscan priest who died at the World Trade Center on 9/11 while ministering as chaplain to the New York City Fire Department.

Diaz, Miguel H., *Queer God de Amor.* Maryknoll, NY: Orbis Books, 2022. A queer theological analysis of the writings of St. John of the Cross, a 16th century Spanish Carmelite mystic.

Farley, RSM, Margaret A. *Just Love: A Framework for Christian Sexual Ethics.* New York: Continuum Press, 2006. Chronicles the history of the church's sexual ethics and presents a new set of criteria, based on the principles of justice and right relationship.

Gramick, Jeannine, and Robert Nugent (Eds.). *Voices of Hope, A Collection of Positive Catholic Writings on Gay and Lesbian Issues.* New York: Center for Homophobia Education, 1995. An anthology of positive statements by Catholic leaders from 1973-1995. Available on the New Ways Ministry website.

Gramick, Jeannine, and Pat Furey (Eds.). The Vatican and Homosexuality, Reactions to the "Letter to the Bishops of the Catholic Church on the Pastoral Care of Homosexual Persons." New York: Crossroad, 1988. An analysis and critique of the Vatican letter, together with pastoral reactions, debate, and responses for future development.

Helminiak, Daniel. *What the Bible* **Really** *Says About Homosexuality.* San Francisco: Alamo Square Press, 1994. The best and most accessible explanation about why the traditional scriptural texts used to condemn homosexuality cannot be accurately applied to lesbian and gay lives today.

Hinze, Christine Firer, and J. Patrick Hornbeck II (Eds.). *More than a Monologue: Sexual Diversity and the Catholic Church. Vol. I: Voices of our Times.* New York: Fordham University Press, 2014. Experiential accounts by LGBTQ Catholics and allies.

Hornbeck II, J. Patrick and Michael A. Norko (Eds.). *More than a Monologue: Sexual Diversity and the Catholic Church. Vol. II: Inquiry, Thought, and Expression.* New York: Fordham University Press, 2014. Explores marriage equality, lesbian nuns, seminary and priesthood life, and bullying of LGBTQ individuals.

Jung, Patricia Beattie and Joseph Andrew Coray, (Eds.). *Sexual Diversity and Catholicism: Toward the Development of Moral Theology.* Collegeville, Minnesota: The Liturgical Press, 2001. An anthology of academic and pastoral essays on lesbian, gay, and bisexual issues.

Jung, Patricia Beattie, and Ralph F. Smith. *Heterosexism: An Ethical Challenge.* Albany: SUNY Press, 1993. This classic text, co-written by a Lutheran and a Catholic, identifies the Christian ethical challenge as heterosexism, not same-sex attraction. It uncovers the biblical and theological roots of Christian heterosexism and proposes a way forward.

Kosnik, Anthony, William Carroll, Agnes Cunningham, Ronald Modras, James Schulte. *Human Sexuality: New Directions in American Catholic Thought.* New York: Paulist Press, 1977. A ground-breaking and readable theological critique of the church's teachings on sexuality based on developments in the natural sciences, social science, and personal experience.

Lopata, Mary Ellen with Casey Lopata. *Fortunate Families: Catholic Families with Lesbian Daughters and Gay Sons.* Victoria, Canada: Trafford Publishing, 2003. An examination of the lives of Catholic parents and relatives of lesbian and gay people based on surveys, questionnaires, and personal interviews.

Martin, SJ, James. *Building a Bridge: How the Catholic Church and the LGBT Community Can Enter into a Relationship of Respect, Compassion, and Sensitivity.* Revised and expanded edition. New York: Harper Collins, 2018. A best-selling book based on the author's acceptance speech when receiving New Ways Ministry's Bridge Building Award. It offers a plan for dialogue between church leaders and LGBTQ people.

McNeill, John. *The Church and the Homosexual.* Kansas City: Sheed, Andrews, and McMeel, 1976. A milestone and first book-length critique of the church's traditional disapproval of lesbian and gay relationships.

Nugent, Robert (Ed.). *A Challenge to Love: Gay and Lesbian Catholics in the Church.* New York: Crossroad, 1983. Essays on social, biblical, theological, pastoral, and vocational perspectives.

Nugent, Robert and Jeannine Gramick. *Building Bridges: Gay and Lesbian Reality and the Catholic Church.* Mystic, Connecticut: Twenty Third Publications, 1992. Essays on education, pastoral ministry, counseling, vowed and clerical life, social concerns, and theological development.

Robinson, Bishop Geoffrey. *Confronting Power and Sex in the Catholic Church: Reclaiming the Spirit of Jesus.* Dublin, Ireland: Columba Press, 2007. A critique of the church's use and misuse of power, particularly in its teachings on sexuality.

Robinson, Bishop Geoffrey. *The 2015 Synod – The Critical Questions: Divorce and Homosexuality.* Australia: ATF Press, 2015. Robinson contends that we "must first look seriously at the church teachings involved to see whether they might allow some 'room to move' in finding pastoral solutions" for the situation of lesbian, gay, bisexual or transgender persons.

Salzman, Todd A., and Michael G. Lawler. *The Sexual Person: Toward a Renewed Catholic Anthropology.* Washington, D.C.: Georgetown University Press, 2008. Critique of sexual ethics, proposal of a person-centered ethic, including lesbian/gay relationships, and new insights on natural law.

Salzman, Todd A., and Michael G. Lawler. *Sexual Ethics: A Theological Introduction*. Washington, D.C.: Georgetown University Press, 2012. Explains why historical developments must be taken into account in developing Catholic moral teaching, including any teaching about lesbian and gay people.

Surdovel IHM, Grace (Ed.). *Love Tenderly: Sacred Stories of Lesbian and Queer Religious*. Mt. Rainier, MD: New Ways Ministry, 2020. Stories by 23 vowed women religious as they explore questions related to the vowed life, falling in love, self-discovery, and acceptance of their sexual identity.

U. S. Bishops' Committee on Marriage and Family. *Always Our Children: A Pastoral Message to Parents of Homosexual Children and Suggestions for Pastoral Ministers*. Washington, DC: United States Catholic Conference, 1997. Offers advice and comfort to Catholic parents and guidance to pastoral ministers.

Booklets

Bouchard OP, Charles (Ed). *Transgender Persons, Their Families and the Church*. St. Louis, MO: Catholic Health Association of the United States, 2020. This booklet contains five personal stories that were presented to the Committee on Doctrine of the U.S. Conference of Catholic Bishops by Catholics who are trans, have trans children, or who minister to trans people. Can be downloaded or ordered in hard copy at https://www.chausa.org/store/products/Product?ID=4492.

DeBernardo, Francis. *Marriage Equality: A Positive Catholic Approach.* Mount Rainier, MD: New Ways Ministry, 2011. Explains why and how Catholics support marriage equality. Available on the New Ways Ministry website.

New Ways Ministry. *Homosexuality: A Positive Catholic Perspective.* Mt. Rainier, MD: New Ways Ministry, 2003. Questions and answers about gay/lesbian life, including pastoral ministry, sexual ethics, civil rights, myths and stereotypes, and the Bible, in an easy to read format. Available on the New Ways Ministry website.

Note: Some older or out of print titles are available at a Catholic university, theologate, seminary library, on the web at www.amazon.com, or at bookstores that sell used books.

Organizations

Bondings 2.0
A daily blog on Catholic LGBTQ news, opinion, and spirituality.
www.NewWaysMinistry.org/blog

Call To Action
A national Catholic social justice organization that includes LGBT justice on its agenda.
www.cta-usa.org

DignityUSA
A national membership organization of LGBTQ Catholics and allies.
www.dignityusa.org

Fortunate Families
A national Catholic ministry comprised of family members, friends, and allies of LGBTQ+ persons.
www.fortunatefamilies.com

Gay, Lesbian, and Straight Education Network (GLSEN)
A national network of teachers and school administrators which strives to assure that each member of every school community is valued and respected regardless of sexual orientation or gender identity/expression.
www.glsen.org

New Ways Ministry
A national ministry that seeks to build bridges of justice, education, advocacy, and dialogue between LGBTQ Catholics and the wider church community.
www.NewWaysMinistry.org

Parents, Families and Friends of Lesbians and Gays (PFLAG)
A national membership organization that celebrates diversity and envisions a society that embraces everyone, including those of diverse sexual orientations and gender identities.
www.pflag.org

Straight Spouse Network
An international organization that provides personal, confidential support and information to heterosexual spouses/partners, current or former, of gay, lesbian, bisexual or transgender mates and mixed-orientation couples for constructively resolving coming-out problems.
www.ourpath.org

Trevor Project
A national organization providing crisis intervention and suicide prevention services to lesbian, gay, bisexual, transgender, queer & questioning (LGBTQ) young people under 25.
www.thetrevorproject.org

Video and Audio Resources

A Two Way Bridge: Fr. James Martin. Mt. Rainier, MD: New Ways Ministry, 2016. 2 hours. A YouTube video of the award ceremony of Fr. James Martin's reception of the Building Bridges Award from New Ways Ministry. Fr. Martin's presentation formed the substance of his book, *Building a Bridge*.
https://www.youtube.com/watch?v=SMcGQS-Faqg&t=5414s

All God's Children: Exploring Homophobia in the African-American Community. San Francisco: WomanVision, 1997. 26 minutes. Parents, politicians, and religious leaders discuss the unique challenges of lesbian and gay people in the African-American community.
www.womanvision.org/all-gods-children.html

Anyone and Everyone. Producer: Agnes Chu. Denver: IronZeal Films, 2007. 57 minutes. Interviews with parents of lesbian, gay, bisexual people from a wide diversity of racial, ethnic, and faith backgrounds. www.ironzeal.com

De Colores: Lesbian and Gay Latinos: Stories of Strength, Family, and Love. Producer: Peter Barbosa. San Francisco: WomanVision, 2001. 28 minutes. Interviews with Latinx parents and their lesbian and gay children.
www.womanvision.org/de-colores.html

Gender Revolution: A Journey with Katie Couric. National Geographic, 2017. 95 minutes. A series of interviews with transgender people, family members, and health professionals that explores new understandings of gender. www.natgeotv.com/ca/gender-revolution or https://www.facebook.com/watch/?v=10154790608436005

Gender: The Space Between. CBSN Originals, March 29, 2017. 30 minutes. Explores the intricate world of gender, transgender narratives, non-binary persons who do not identify as a man or a woman. These are some of their stories.
https://www.youtube.com/watch?v=ZFWrzw9szt8

How Pope Francis Is Changing the Vatican's Tone on LGBT People. New York: America Media, Nov. 18, 2021. 10 minutes. Description of events that show how the Vatican's approach has changed, by Colleen Dulle; along with an interview with Fr. James Martin, SJ, about that change.
https://www.youtube.com/watch?v=rrslGK0kls4

In Good Conscience: Sister Jeannine Gramick's Journey of Faith. Producer: Barbara Rick. New York: Out of The Blue Films, 2004. 60 minutes. A documentary about New Ways Ministry's co-founder, her decades-long ministry with the LGBTQ community, and her struggle with the Vatican. www.ingoodconscience.com/

LGBT Catholics: Owning Our Faith. Producer: Out at St. Paul's, New York, 2015. 15 minutes. Interviews by a New York parish ministry.
www.owningourfaith.com/welcome

Living Our Marianist Charism: Embracing the LGBTQ+ Community. An exploration of how the U.S. Marianist community is ministering with LGBTQ+ people. Marianist Social Justice Collaborative, 2020. 11 minutes.

My Brother Dan: A Talk with Parents by Bishop Thomas Gumbleton. Delivered at a retreat for parents in Connecticut, October 7, 1995, this 90-minute listening program concludes with a brief interview by the National Public Radio with Bishop Gumbleton.
www.newwaysministry.org/family/

Outreach 2021. America Media. New York: June 26, 2021. 4 minutes. Highlights from speakers at a conference on LGBTQ Catholic Ministry.
https://www.youtube.com/watch?v=o11V7ep_2KI

PRIDE. A seven-minute video with student interviews about being LGBT at St. Vincent's, a Catholic college in Pennsylvania. https://youtu.be/1TmKLfgzczw

Straight from the Heart. Producer: Dee Mosbacher. San Francisco: WomanVision, 1994. 22 minutes. This documentary, featuring interviews with parents of lesbian and gay people from a variety of back-grounds, was nominated for an Academy Award.
www.womanvision.org/straight-from-the-heart.html

What Happens in a Christian Family when a Child Comes Out as Homosexual? Producer: Gionata News. Italy. 10 minutes. YouTube interview with four sets of Italian parents. English subtitles. Parents discuss "How did your-family experience coming out"? and "What would you say to a parent who has just found out their child is gay or lesbian"?
https://www.youtube.com/watch?v=vU62suliiA0&feature=youtu.be

"What's 'Gay'?" Asked Mae. Producer: Mark Schoen. Illustrator: Dave Woodford. Delightful, 3-minute animated movie for youngsters, based on Brian McNaught's book of the same name. Close-captions, Spanish subtitles.
www.sexsmartfilms.com

About the Authors

Andrea Baghi and Silvia Donati are Catholic parents who belong to 3volteGenitori (3timesParents), a network of parents who have LGBT children.

Fr. Gian Luca Carrega is director of the Office for Pastoral Care of Cultures of the Diocese of Turin, Italy, and, on mandate from his archbishop, he manages pastoral activities for LGBT people and their families.

Corrado Contini and Michela Munari are members of Gruppo Davide, a group of Catholic parents of LGBT children, and 3volteGenitori, an Italian network of Christian parents of LGBT children.

Francis DeBernardo has been the Executive Director of New Ways Ministry since 1996. He is the Editor of *Bondings 2.0,* a daily blog on Catholic LGBTQ news, opinion, and spirituality.

Marisa Delmonte and Angelo Donati are the parents of Silvia Donati, their lesbian daughter. They are part of AGESCI and the Focolare movement.

Gianni Geraci is a volunteer of the Guado Group, the oldest Italian group of gay and lesbian believers founded in Milan in 1980. Between 1996 and 2006 he was the spokesperson for the Coordination of Christian Homosexual Groups in Italy, the first attempt to create an Italian network dealing with faith and homosexuality.

Jeannine Gramick is a Sister of Loretto who taught mathematics before she was assigned by her religious leaders to full time ministry on behalf of LGBTQ people. She and Fr. Robert Nugent co-founded New Ways Ministry in 1977.

Mara Grassi and Agostino Usai are part of the group for families of LGBT Catholics in Regina Pacis Parish in Reggio Emilia and the Davide Group in Parma. They are joint vice-presidents of La Tenda di Gionata, an association for parents and families of LGBT Catholics.

Serenella Longarini and Salvatore Olmetto have three daughters, one of whom is lesbian. For several years, they have been engaged in a parish as catechists and animators.

Dea Santonico is the mother of a young gay man. She is a member of Comunita' di Base di San Paolo in Rome and of Parola e parole, a group of parents, relatives and friends of LGBT persons, formed upon the initiative of the Cammini di Speranza association, a network of Italian LGBT Christian organizations.

LA TENDA di GIONATA

ODV-ETS

accogliere formare e informare su fede e omosessualità

Jonathan's Tent

La Tenda di Gionata (Jonathan's Tent) is an Italian organization that was established in 2018 to support LGBT people. It was founded by Father David Esposito, a curate of Illice, a small parish and community in Central Italy

Father David Esposito probably read very carefully the following words of Pope Francis from an interview with Father Antonio Spadaro, SJ, on August 19, 2013.

> *"The Church, sometimes, has been cornered in small things and petty commandments."*
>
> -Pope Francis

Surely Father Esposito remembered these words of Pope Francis when, bedridden and terminally ill, he called the volunteers of Progetto Gionata and asked them to continue the group that was gathering on the internet.

Father Esposito wanted to help LGBT people, their parents, and the Church's pastors to build a bridge of dialogue and reciprocal listening. He wanted the churches to be "ever more sanctuaries of welcoming and support for LGBT people and all others who suffer discrimination."

Thus Jonathan's Tent (La Tenda di Gionata) was born. This non-profit organization welcomes, educates, and informs LGBT Christians, their families, pastoral workers and, most of all, Christian communities, to support LGBT people and victims of any form of discrimination.

As the Pastoral Constitution on the Church in the Modern World (*Gaudium et Spes*) states: "*The joys and the hopes, the grief and the anguish of the people of our time, especially of those who are poor or in any way afflicted, are the joys and hopes, the grief and anguish of the followers of Christ as well*" (par. 1).

To learn more about Gionata, visit the website:
www.gionata.org/tenda-di-gionata-english-news/

To support one of Gionata's projects contact:
tendadigionata@gmail.com

New Ways Ministry

Mission

New Ways Ministry provides a positive ministry of education and advocacy for lesbian, gay, bisexual, trans-gender and queer (LGBTQ) Catholics within the larger Christian and civil communities. New Ways Ministry fosters dialogue, strives to eradicate homophobia and transphobia, and promotes the acceptance of LGBTQ people as full and equal members of church and society.

History

Founded in 1977 by Sister Jeannine Gramick, SSND and Father Robert Nugent, SDS, New Ways Ministry takes its name from the pastoral letter of Bishop Francis Mugavero, *Sexuality: God's Gift*, in which the Bishop said, "...*we pledge our willingness ...to try to find **new ways** to communicate the truth of Christ because we believe it will make you free.*" (Feb. 11, 1976)

The Call of the Church

"If a person is gay and seeks out the Lord and is willing, who am I to judge?"
                    -Pope Francis, July 29, 2013

Programs

New Ways Ministry consists of a Board of Directors, an Advisory Board, professional program staff, and volunteers. Some of the programs include:

> -a daily blog of Catholic LGBTQ news, opinion, and spirituality, as well as a quarterly newsletter,

-networking nationally and internationally with other Catholic or LGBTQ religious organizations,

-retreats for LGBTQ persons, their families and allies,

-pilgrimages for LGBTQ-friendly persons to major sites of Christian history,

-publication and distribution of books, articles, and other resources,

-public statements on current issues involving LGBTQ Catholics and the institutional Church,

-symposiums for Church leaders about theological developments and pastoral practices,

-Bridge Building Awards to individuals for outstanding contributions to LGBTQ issues in the Catholic Church,

- programs for and about parents, parishes, schools, campus ministers, theologians, transgender persons, gay priests and brothers, and lesbian nuns,

-Fr. Robert Nugent Memorial Lectures in memory of New Ways Ministry's co-founder.

Contact

4012 29th Street, Mount Rainier, MD 20712, USA
301-277-5674
info@NewWaysMinistry.org
www:NewWaysMinistry.org

Printed in Great Britain
by Amazon